I0490019

Online Marketing for Start-ups and Offline Business

By Ade Asefeso MCIPS MBA

Copyright 2014 by Ade Asefeso MCIPS MBA
All rights reserved.

Second Edition

ISBN-13: 978-1499656497

ISBN-10: 1499656491

Publisher: AA Global Sourcing Ltd
Website: http://www.aaglobalsourcing.com

Table of Contents

Disclaimer

This publication is designed to provide competent and reliable information regarding the subject matter covered. However, it is sold with the understanding that the author and publisher are not engaged in rendering professional advice. The authors and publishers specifically disclaim any liability that is incurred from the use or application of contents of this book.

If you purchased this book without a cover you should be aware that this book may have been stolen property and reported as "unsold and destroyed" to the publisher. In this case neither the author nor the publisher has received any payment for this "stripped book."

Dedication

This book is dedicated to the hundreds of thousands of incredible souls in the world who have weathered through the up and down of recent recession.

To my family and friends who seems to have been sent here to teach me something about who I am supposed to be. They have nurtured me, challenged me, and even opposed me…. But at every juncture has taught me!

This book is dedicated to my lovely boys, Thomas, Michael and Karl. Teaching them to manage their finance will give them the lives they deserve. They have taught me more about life, presence, and energy management than anything I have done in my life.

Chapter 1: Introduction

Back in 2006 I became interested in marketing and advertising quite by accident. I was employed by a major high tech company as Sales and Operations Director. When a new product for analyzing the effectiveness of various advertising campaigns was installed, I was expected to learn the product and then teach the marketing gurus how to use it.

I was fascinated with demographics and how campaigns were deployed. I considered changing my career and going back to school but got side tracked with a cross-country move, however I studied MBA Marketing Module after finishing my MBA in 2006 just for the fun of it! .

Let's look at what I was considering then compared to what the market looks like now. My company was spending a lot of money on advertising campaigns that were done on TV, in direct mail, flyers on door handles, inserts into the monthly bill, etc. All of these were the traditional form of advertising we were using then. From what I saw of these advertising campaigns, there were more losers than there were successes. However, when the successes are huge, it masks the losses. Customers today are more savvy and are just plain tired of all the junk mail whether it paper or electronic.

Online marketing, also called Internet Marketing, still uses demographics as well as several other factors to target the consumer. A major difference here can be in the dollar/pounds amount spent on these campaigns. Many businesses are still creating commercial web sites that were simply online brochures and product catalogues. Customers would check out what they wanted but many were afraid to give credit card information online so they just placed the call instead. Because of the new encryption technology, customers feel more confident with online purchases. The number of internet users today is 1996 million or 28.7% of the world population. Compare that to August of 2001 when it was 513 million, 8.6% of the world population. That means it 4 times bigger in just 10 years! If you like statistics (and I do) consider that Sweden has the highest percentage (73.6%) of their people on the internet and the United States is at 68.5%. If this does not get you excited about online marketing, I am not sure what would.

Online marketing has a completely different set of tools it uses for marketing. Search engine marketing, joint ventures, opt-in emails, newsletters, etc. Each type of campaign can reach a different type of prospective client depending on how you decide to run the particular campaign. I will cover each of these later in this book.

Many of the pioneers of online marketing who saw this potential are now exceedingly wealthy. If you check online, you will see that several of them are producing eBooks and eCourses that detail the 'secrets of internet success." Quite often these books and courses are distributed via download for free. With this kind of information available, there has never been a better time to start an online business or market your current offline business online. Here is to your future success.

Chapter 2: The Secrets of Internet and Online Marketing

You probably already use the Online World for many things. Whether you use it for entertainment, research, sending E-mail to friends and family, or just discussing numerous subject topics with others.

Of all the things you can do online, there is one that you should definitely know how to do. MARKET A BUSINESS ONLINE!

That's right, with the power of the Online World to reach millions of people, Online Marketing is definitely an awesome tool that no business should be without. The simple fact that advertising is practically FREE. The ability to get the results of thousands of dollars in free publicity is practically unheard of in business today. Only recently have more and more people figured out how to utilize the ever exploding Online World to market their business efforts.

Think about it, there is probably no business in existence that could not benefit from free publicity! And the fact that properly utilizing free advertising raises net profits to unbelievable levels! Using any or all of the major online services, or the INTERNET, can help you market your business efforts.

Let's start with plain-old advertising. On America Online, for example, they will let you place classified advertisements for FREE! They have a variety of classifications to choose from. By placing these small free ads you can generate some very quality leads that can turn into sales. Or if you are a really good marketer you could sell something straight from your free ad. Wouldn't that be something, using the actual free ad to do all of the selling?

The other services offer free advertising from time to time. When they do charge for classified ads it is usually very inexpensive, and still a great deal considering how many people those ads can reach. When you place any advertisements you should always "code" your ads. This means put something in each individual ad that will tell you, if you get any business from it, which ad it came from. This way, you will probably find that some sections are better producers than others, and you will want to concentrate on these sections and not the ones that were not making any money.

To code an ad you could make them request a certain "report" for more information. You should give each report a different code for each ad. Such as: "ask for report number 1 TV", this way you would know that this request came from the ad on television, for sale category, and so forth. If they send you an order straight from the ad, make them give you an order number, which would be different for each ad. THE MAJORITY OF PEOPLE WHO ARE ADVERTISING ONLINE ARE NOT USING THESE AD CODES!!! THIS IS A MAJOR MARKETING MISTAKE!!!

By not tracking exactly which ads are making money, they are wasting their time by continually placing ads in "loser" categories. The actual code can be anything you want to assign to it. ALWAYS keep track of every ad you place. Make a note of what it said, where and when it was placed. You will be pleasantly surprised when you analyze your "ad data" and see some positive trends developing. Just repeat these trends and it will help you to make more money!

How would you like to find a name list of several hundred (or even thousands) people who might be interested in the particular product or service you are selling based on their jobs or interests? Wouldn't that be great!? Well, you can! And the Online Services supply this service as a part of your regular membership.

This little unknown tool is called the "Member Directory!" You can do searches in the directory for other users with certain characteristics. For example, if you were selling fishing equipment, you could do a search by "fishing." All of the people that were registered in the directory and had listed fishing as one of their hobbies would show up on that search list. You could now send each one of those people an e-mail message telling them about your product or service, it is just like using a mailing list, but you have no postage! (*Make sure you check with your online service to see if they allow unsolicited E-mail.)

You can also get the names of several prospects by doing some "browsing" in the different topic forums.

Using the earlier example of looking for people who fish, you could look under sports until you found a discussion on fishing. You could then take note of the users' names that were participating in the discussions. You could do the same thing on the INTERNET with one of the many newsgroup topics that they have.

The bottom line is that you 'test" and record the results of your Online Marketing efforts. Then just repeat the steps that are making you money and expand on them to reach more people.

Doing simple research on the Internet. The Internet has several mailing lists that are dedicated to marketing on the Internet. You will also find hundreds of articles on the World Wide Web. By searching one of the WWW search engines like WebCrawler you can find all the information you can read. Use search strings such as: "online marketing", "internet advertising", 'selling online", and so on.

You can also find many books on the subject at your local bookstore or being advertised online.

Chapter 3: Marketing your Online Home Business

Home businesses, like other businesses, are not successful just because they exist. If you want to work at home, you have to learn about marketing a home based business.

Marketing depends in large part on the type of business you have. Marketing on the internet works for most kinds of home business. Even if you plan the bulk of your business from your local area, a website adds professionalism. When sending emails, make sure you include information about your business in your signature file.

If you own a website or other business on the internet, you need customers. With all the competing websites, how do they find you?

You need to have some good strategies for marketing an online business. One of the most used strategies for marketing a home business is learning to get a high search engine ranking. If you do not rank highly you may have difficulty being found.

There are some key methods for high ranking. Start by keeping everything on your site relevant to the subject. This makes good sense anyway because once the customer has found you, you want him to stick around. Choose a domain name and website title that fit well with your business keywords. Your title should be easy to remember. Links to your website make a difference in search engine rankings, so contact sites that offer information complementing yours and ask for reciprocal links. Be aware that this information can change as search engines redesign their methods for relevant results.

Another strategy for marketing an online business is to use pay-per-click advertising. This can be a fast way to get listed high in the search engines. There are several providers of pay-per-click advertising. It pays to check out a variety to see which suits your needs the best.

Blogs are a newer source for marketing an online business. They tend to rank well, and consumers like them. Use your blog to talk about your industry and provide links to your website. Blogs add a lot to your marketing program and can be fun to write.

An often overlooked tool for marketing a home based business is staying in touch with former clients. You can do this through the phone or through email. Email is often the preferred choice because potential clients look at email when they have time and are not interrupted to do it, as they are on the phone. When emailing former clients, let them know you enjoyed working with them and want them to remember you for future projects.

Look for ways to meet potential customers. Go to trade meetings or conventions. For example, if you are selling pet products, attend dog shows and county fairs.

The major ways to for marketing an online business are similar to other businesses. Find customers you can serve and find ways to let them know you exist. After they become clients, serve them well and ask for future business. This is how you keep your business running.

Marketing a home business is essential for success. Use all the marketing strategies at your disposal and watch your traffic grow.

Chapter 4: Marketing Online with Organic Search Engine Optimization

Basically, marketing is about helping customers/ prospects find your website/business - looking to grow your business, increase sales leads, or lower customer acquisition costs. You have already read about other ways to do that, but smart marketing means you will use a combination of both search engine optimization and pay per click. Call it online search engine advertising if you will - it works and generates new business.

To be even more specific: organic search engine optimization is the process of optimizing a web site or page so it ranks well in the free listings of the search engines. This is the best (and least expensive) option for getting visitors. Why?

Visitors click on free organic listings more often than paid listings. Something else you need to know so you realize just how important this is for your site. Just about 65% of business websites were created solely for customers without any search engine optimization. Translation: two thirds of businesses on the web are in the bottom of engine results. Since approximately 85% of online sales come from search engine traffic – you have got a problem. Without getting into too much detail about "how-to" accomplish this organic optimization - suffice it to say the methods are called "White Hat" and involve keyword research, key phrase placement in your Meta tags and content, and the application of special formatting such as headers, bold and bullets. Remember to do both online AND offline optimization. This includes regularly submitting to directories, writing press releases, submitting articles, and getting other links pointing back to your site. To get relevant links - start a blog about your key phrase. Link from it to your web site, and keep the content on both fresh and original. The good news? 70% of search engine users visit organic sites, and 50% of them select the top results. Imagine what that will mean for your marketing site.

Google AdWords offers you:

Targeted reach: Now you can advertise to people searching on Google. Even if you already appear in Google's search results, AdWords can help you target new audiences on Google and our advertising network.

Greater control: You can edit your ads and adjust your budget until you get the results you want. You can also display a variety of ad formats and even target your ads to specific languages and geographic locations.

Measurable value: There is no minimum spending requirement or time commitment. And with the cost-per-click option, you are only charged if people click your ads. This means every dollar/pounds of your budget goes toward bringing new prospects to you.

Local and regional targeting Set your ads to appear

only to people searching in a particular region. Now it's easy to target online customers within, say, 25 miles of your front door.

Get noticed on Google Maps. People searching for information related to your business will see your location, contact information, and an image of your choosing highlighted on a map of your area.

Chapter 5: Article Marketing Benefits Online Retailers

Strategically developing online content helps to ensure a small-business owner's success in both the short and long term.

Article marketing is a smart, comprehensive way to broaden the online presence of your small business enterprise. By posting articles to ezines, directories and newsletters, you can reap benefits ranging from new clients and a solid reputation to increased website traffic and heightened visibility.

At the heart of most successful article marketing is a comprehensive strategy known as Search Engine Optimization, a process through which keyword rich documents are published online to help to improve website traffic.

Online marketers using search engine optimization (SEO) techniques choose a keyword or phrase that people will likely search for when conducting research. They then create relevant, engaging articles throughout which the critical word or phrase is used. Once these documents are posted online, search engines add them to their immense cache of information which helps to strategically drive traffic to selected websites. In addition to keyword rich document publishing, though, a second critical component of an online marketing strategy must include the distribution of a given website's URL.

Publishing a website's address at the end of SEO articles will allow interested readers to easily visit the site by clicking on the embedded link.

When executed with quality, a useful article that is correctly formatted and well written, can provide a free way to quickly strengthen your online presence. Seek out a few places to post your articles. There are many free article directories and e-zines that actively request informative articles on any number of given topics. These resources are important allies when developing successful article marketing strategies.

Online article marketing, however, does more than simply heighten your internet visibility. Unlike direct paid advertising, it actually presents an opportunity to educate and assist your customer base. By providing useful resources online, you can make a case that benefits your business while building a reputation as an authoritative and knowledgeable entity. Further, article marketing offers a longer lasting form of promoting your business than does standard advertising alone. Paid ads usually lose potency and relevance over time. But a well-written, useful article will acquire hits and encourage viral marketing for months at a time.

Additionally, article marketing is one of the few forms of promotion that have the potential to reach a large audience without considerable financial investment and it is unique because it empowers you to position a nuanced message prominently in the vast landscape of the web. You can reach customers who you would have no access to you otherwise and the cost is typically measured in time rather than dollars.

Article marketing offers significant numbers of benefits to retailers who choose to engage in the strategic method of search engine optimization. For many small business in particular, it is the best way to use the power of the internet to bring prospective clients to your door. Importantly, the most successful marketing campaigns understand that quality, content and keyword relevancy are critical components of good marketing. Therefore, investing the time to ensure you develop great ideas, witty content and informative articles will help you reap the greatest benefit of article marketing in both the short and long term.

Chapter 6: Business Marketing Online

Many people are starting Online Businesses, but learning on the fly, so to speak, how to get traffic to their sites. A big factor to be considered is how much will it cost to get the traffic to your web site. I recently wrote two articles, one about specific landing pages and the second about matching keywords to specific landing pages. This time I am going to cover the cost of each keyword. In other words how much should you pay for each phrase or keyword?

You can recognize the demand for online business by looking at the searches made on the search engines. They are phrases like business conferencing meeting online web, advertising business online web, business free online site web, online web business opportunity, business hosting online page web, online business web hosting and business create online site web opportunity just to mention a few.

There is much that is to be learned about this topic and I am only going to scratch the surface in this book, but it should get you started off correctly. There are many factors to consider that can make a big difference in your profit.

You should ensure that you have a different landing page on your site for each area of you business. For example see www.aaglobalsourcing.com

If you are utilizing one of the tools available to us called (PPC) Paid Per Click Advertising, whereby we pay a search engine pennies to show our ad when someone types in particular keyword. As I mentioned earlier in this book you must break up your keywords in such a manner as to have all of your keywords on a given topic sent to the specific landing page. For example you should have all Work At Home keywords go to your landing page, which is mostly about Work At Home ideas. Like wise have your keywords on Home Based Business go to the landing page that highlights Home Based Business Opportunities.

In addition you do not want to bidding against yourself so you want to make sure that you do not mix and match your keywords. You will want to advertise only the keywords that match a specific landing page when using (PPC) Paid Per Click Advertising. Do not have Work At Home keywords mixed in with Online Paid Surveys sending people to multiple landing Pages.

You will want to use multiple variation of a given keyword. Think about the conversation going on in your customer's head. What would you type in if you were searching for the same thing? What would others type? Don't just set you campaigns to run on a maximum price per click. Do some research to see how much a particular keyword is being searched for. If it is not one of the most popular decrease you bid amount. Once you have done this monitor it over a couple of weeks or a month so you can see if you are getting the same amount of clicks.

Search engines are not always going to give you the best price. Some of the big ones are pretty fair, but I want control of these things myself. Many of my keywords are half the price of some of the major ones. Before I learned this though, many search engines were charging me full price when it was not warranted.

Every subtle change in your website landing page, keywords, keyword bidding, no matter how minuscule, has an effect on your customer. I always recommend change, monitor, analyze, modify and keep continuing the process. Compare the new change to the old one so that you can see which landing page converts best.

Once you have had your website going for awhile there is always much more fine tuning to do.

Feel free to contact us via.
http://www.qualitywebdesign.aaglobalsourcing.com/ contact-quality-web-desig if you would like coaching on SEO or help on how to use online marketing for your offline business or search engine optimize of your existing website. Your feedback is important to me.

Chapter 7: Why Choose Affiliate Marketing as your Online Business

There are many online businesses coming out today. You might have seen a website selling ebooks or different kinds of services. With so many online businesses coming out with selling the same products, these businesses cannot succeed with proper advertising.

This is where you come in. You can offer to advertise for them or sign up as an affiliate.

An affiliate program works by giving you a commission for every product they sold to every referral you directed to their website. Some affiliate programs will offer pay per click.

This means that if a visitor from your website clicks the link or banner of the company you posted in your site, they will pay you, if different people or users of your website make the clicks.

Since there are so many online businesses wanting to sign up websites as an affiliate, you will never run out of clients. There will always be new online businesses that will open up. If you do affiliate marketing right, you will never lose.

Affiliate marketing can be such a great business, especially for people who are considering starting an online business at home. With good internet traffic, your earnings in affiliate programs can be enough to make ends meet.

Affiliate marketing is a great business for every type of people. Whether you are an average person with a regular job or a student who wants to make extra cash or whether if you are a stay at home parent who wants to help with the household expenses, affiliate marketing is perfect for everyone.

Affiliate marketing allows you to start your home business right away.

All you need is a website and an investment of a little time, a little effort and a little money to get good internet traffic in your website. Sometimes if you are good in promoting your website, you need to invest no money at all.

Here are some of the reasons why affiliate marketing can be a great business:

To start with, you need no actual products or services to sell. Most people start their online business selling products or services; this can lead to spending more money, depending on what type of product or service they sell.

In affiliate marketing, all you have to do is create a website with specific topic and post a link of your affiliate that sells products or services that is relevant to your website topic. For example, you can create a website that discusses health insurance. You then put up a link in your website of other websites that sells different kinds of health insurance.

Depending on what kind of website you set up, you need no actual customer service. This means you have no need to employ people, therefore, saving money for salary and of course, office space.

You are your own boss. In addition, since that is the case, you get to choose what website you want to sign up as an affiliate. Remember that you have to choose a business that suits your website.

Affiliate marketing can give you lots of free time. What you need to do is just set up your website, advertise it and set up your affiliate program. After that, you have all the time in the world to do what ever pleases you.

However, you should also check your website and update it from time to time to keep visitors interested in your website. For example, your affiliate's products have upgraded, you also need to update your topics regarding the new features and products.

Once you have a good amount of internet traffic and subscriber list, you become an affiliate magnet. Businesses who depend largely on affiliate marketing to promote internet traffic to their website will often offer you to sign up for them as an affiliate. Sometimes, some businesses will even offer you a bonus by just signing you up as an affiliate.

These are just some of the reasons why affiliate

marketing is a great business. There are many possibilities in affiliate marketing. All you have to do is be creative in promoting your website. Try to advertise your website by writing articles and posting them in article publishing websites, this is a great way to increase targeted internet traffic in your website.

In addition, keep in mind that internet traffic means more visitors who will likely buy the products your affiliate program is promoting.

For you to be successful in this field, make your website as attractive as possible. You not only have to get good web traffic but you also need keep visitors coming back again.

Chapter 8: Increasing Online Sales through Affiliate Marketing

One of the most tried, trusted, and beneficial ways of increasing online sales through marketing and advertising is affiliate marketing. This is basically a revenue share sort of system, where an affiliate is given a form of commission from a merchant, based on how many sales the affiliate has generated through advertising on his or her site. Affiliate marketing began just four years after the world-wide web was launched, and many successful e-commerce sites owe much to this simple yet effective method.

There are three types of affiliate marketing methods of payment – either pay-per-click (generated by actual clicks or referrals to the merchant from the affiliate's site), pay-per-action or pay-per-sale (very similar, in that the affiliate receives payment, either a fixed amount or commission, based on the sales or subscriptions that have come through referrals or adverts on the affiliate's site.) The last two methods of payment are generally preferred by merchants, due to many fraudsters taking advantage of the click system and setting up sites with forced clicks, pop-ups, adware, spam, false advertising and many other "black hat" techniques.

Affiliate marketing is not limited to only display-adverts on an affiliate site, but also comes in the form of email, blogs, rss feeds, content and niche sites, loyalty sites, comparison sites or shopping directories, and other forms. It is an extremely low cost, but highly effective form of marketing and advertising, presenting little to no risk for both the merchant and the affiliate.

Chapter 9: Affiliate Marketing - the Stepchild of Online Marketing

The real step-child of online marketing is affiliate marketing, a tried and trusted method for creating sales and advertising websites or products online. Many e-commerce sites owe a great deal to affiliate marketing methods – namely Amazon.com and CDNOW's WebBuy system. Affiliate marketing is a highly efficient way to create brand awareness and generate leads and business.

Affiliate marketing encourages "affiliates" to sell or advertise a merchant's products by means of a revenue share or commission system. In the early days of the web when affiliate marketing started (about late 1994) most merchants made use of a Cost-Per-Click system (known as CPC or CPM) where an affiliate made money from every click to the merchant's website generated from the affiliate's site. Because of bad management and many fraudsters taking advantage of this system in various ways, only about 1% of affiliate marketing is now done this way. 80% of affiliate marketing is now on a cost-per-sale basis, where the affiliate receives commission for every actual SALE generated on the merchant's site that is due to a referral from the affiliate – and the last 19% of affiliate marketing is on a cost-per-action basis, where the affiliate receives a revenue-share if the person referred from their site actually subscribes or registers with the merchant's website.

Affiliate marketing is done through different types of techniques or publisher websites - blogs and RSS feeds becoming quite a predominant method, as well as shopping and comparison websites, loyalty websites and others.

Chapter 10: Blog Marketing Online: what you Should Know

Marketing your blog online can get complicated and confusing if you are working on your first one. However, for a blog marketing guru, it really is not that complicated. Anyone that is familiar with blog marketing online knows that it takes dedication, hard work and consistency. For someone just starting out with their marketing campaign, it may seem like a lot of work with little or no pay off to be seen right afterwards. However, just know that marketing is something that you have to build. You have to work on it and continue to market your blog.

There are many things that you can do to market your blog and get it out there to be seen by the world. One of the most important things is to visit other blogs that are relevant to yours and leave comments. Doing so gets your blog out there to readers of other's blogs. And in return can get you some new visitors as well as readers. While all of this might seem confusing at first, after a while you will get the hang of it and it will make sense and fall in place.

Posting on your blog on a regular basis is another way to get new readers. Who wants to read a blog that is never even updated? Would you? Of course not! So give your readers what they want with new content and give it to them often. Post daily, weekly or bi weekly and be consistent about it. This way your readers and visitors will know how often to check your blog for a new post.

Know where your traffic is coming from. Know which search engines are directing people to your blog and which are not. Find out what keywords are bringing people to your blog as well. If you know all of this all ready, use it to your advantage. Write more content on the keywords that are working for you and monitor where you fall on the search engine pages that are sending visitors.

If someone leaves a comment on your blog, be sure to acknowledge it. No one wants to have a conversation with themselves, and it will only take a brief moment to reply and let them know you appreciate them. Otherwise if you have a section full of comments and you have not replied, chances are that you will not be getting many more. The readers may even drop you off of their list of blogs to visit frequently as well. Using your head and treating others as you would want to be treated is a big part of marketing.

Make friends with other bloggers. Network with them and find out how they get so many visitors to their blog and what they do to keep them interested. Exchanging ideas with other bloggers that are successful is a great idea and a good way to make friends. If you want, you can even become friends with other bloggers offline as well. Use this to your advantage and do not just take from the conversation though, be sure that you share all of your blog marketing techniques as well with your new found blogging friends.

If you happen to be quoting an article from another source or blog, always be sure to provide a link back to the original. Other wise this is known as plagiarism and something that is looked down on in the world of marketing. Stealing someone else's content is not a good idea and not something that you will get away with. You will get caught if you try to say someone else's work is your own of it is not. This is not a good way to start off in the blog marketing world as well.

Blog marketing is a great way to make extra income and get your blog out there and known. Use these techniques above to get your blog more traffic and readers and you will eventually reap the rewards.

Chapter 11: Creating Online Marketing Business Opportunity

Within this article on creating online marketing business opportunities, we will look at ways that you are able to build your online business through online marketing. There are many different ways that you can go around this so we will look at a couple of very good and low-cost ways to do this.

One of the best ways that you are able to market online at a low cost is through giveaways. You can do this in many different ways but one the best ways is to go to free forums and post that you have free giveaways at your website. You will want your giveaway item to be very low cost. By keeping costs low, you can post to these forums on a regular basis and receive steady traffic which can help you build your website. You will be generating a great deal of traffic for yourself at a very low cost. There are many different ways to run a sweepstakes or a giveaways contest but many websites will have giveaways pursuant upon the fact that you sign up for their newsletter. Make sure that the people who sign up are ones that you want to target because your newsletter can be your greatest source of marketing.

Another great way that you can bring about more traffic to your website is through Adwords. Adwords is a form of advertising that is run by Google where you are allowed to bid on certain keywords that people search for. You can run your marketing using a budget and you will know that you are getting the target audience that you want towards your website. One of the ways that you can work at saving and maintaining a budget using Adwords is to log into your Google account every day to see how much it is costing you to use your keywords. By looking at how much it costs for keywords, you can make sure that your marketing budget is right on track with what you should be. You can also get an idea as to trends developing with the costs of Adwords. Alternatively we can let you advertise your products and services on one of our websites already on page 1 of google organically, these is far cheaper than google pay per click and it is likely to be visited by potential customer, Feel free to contact us via http://www.qualitywebdesign.aaglobalsourcing.com/ contact-quality-web-desig if you would like us to help on how to use online marketing for your offline business or search engine optimize of your existing website. Your feedback is important to me.

Hopefully this book will help you build your business. A different angle on creating online marketing business opportunities is spotlighted now. There is a great deal of unused advertising out there which could be bought up at discounts on what online advertising firms normally charge. If you were able to find a great deal of this unused advertising and buy it at a discount, you could resell it to other companies looking to put more of their advertising out online and charge them a higher price. This is often known as advertising arbitrage where you buy the ad spots at a discount and then resell them at a slightly higher price but making sure that the people who ultimately by your ads are getting a very good discount. All parties win in this particular engagement. This gives you something to think about the next time that you see empty spaces on a website's home page!

Chapter 12: Creating Marketing for a Business

Each business is different and the type of marketing that it will do online so you want to find some way test enough from their competition. This is a general rule no matter what type of business you are possibly looking into, whether it be offline or online.

One of the great ways that can work in creating marketing for a business can actually be run from your website. Develop a forum or discussion board on which different topics of importance to your customers are listed. People will want to come back again and again to read what others have to say and this provides you with some great repeat traffic. This can help your natural search engine traffic in getting your page is indexed as well as provide some back link opportunities, which will help in marketing your online business. Within your forum, you are able to create marketing of some sort because it is your website. When these customers are ready to buy, they will think of buying from you first because of the connection between your website and them. Within this way, you have created a win-win situation for both parties. You will have developed a stable base of customers while also giving yourself the opportunity to grow your business due to the opportunities listed such as back links, search engine traffic, and being more heavily indexed.

Another good way to help in creating marketing for

an online business is to give away free products. You can advertise your free giveaways in many of the freebie forums that can be found around the Internet. There is great traffic to these websites and if you are able to divert some of this to your website, you will be much the better for it. If you are using free giveaways, make sure that you are receiving something in return such as the person's e-mail address because they have signed up for your newsletter. When you are using giveaways as a form of advertising, you will want to make sure that you are able to get some sort of return on your investment so keep this in mind when posting to the freebie forums.

The final way in which I will look at creating marketing for a business is to write good sales copy. This is going to be one of the simplest methods for you will quite possibly the most effective because my improving what is written on your website, you will be able to convert more of your traffic and this will have a direct impact on your bottom line.

 Each of these three ways of creating marketing for an online business can be very effective. By taking the time to improve your website, you will find that this will have the greatest impact upon your bottom line of running a website and an Internet business. If your website does not run effectively and draw customers in, then going out and working on bringing traffic in is a lost cause.

Chapter 13: Creating Online Business Marketing

Throughout these book we have looked at many different ways that one can create online business ideas. This is very important but it is equally important that you know how to market your business ideas so that people know what you have to offer. Within this book we are going to look at what you can do in creating online business marketing that will sell your product. We will look at two different methods that you can use but, to truly become successful at online marketing, you are going to have to make sure to learn about the subject as much as possible. Without a certain number of hits to your website every day, you can be guaranteed that you will not have great sales figures. The only way to get the hits that you want is through marketing and this is where this book comes in.

The first thing you can do in creating online business marketing is to make sure that your website is properly created. This book is not long enough to go into everything that you need for your website but you should make sure that your site is properly indexed by all of the major search engines so that you are getting the maximum amount of natural search engine traffic you can. If you need help on this feel free to contact us via. http://www.qualitywebdesign.aaglobalsourcing.com/contact-quality-web-desig Your feedback is important to me. We can help you redesign some pages on your website to make sure that you are getting maximum exposure.

Chapter 14: Email Marketing and Opt- in List Building

Since the advent of the information technology, the Internet had been a valuable commodity to most people. Here, they find ways on how to earn more money even without having to spend more capital on building a business.

Nowadays, many business people are realizing the importance of email marketing. Through emails, an online business can market their product directly through their customers.

Generally, the main purpose of email marketing is to reach their target audience as quickly and as direct as possible. They need to reach their target market so as to promote their products and services that would benefit their customers.

However, some businesses use email marketing in order to maintain their contact and relationship with their customers.

The reason why email marketing has grown in such unprecedented rate is based on the fact that people in the virtual community are always hungry for information. They subscribe to information that they are interested in.

On the other hand, not all people are willing to subscribe to such information. They may be interested on your products once but may no longer be interested to buy again. Moreover, when you continue to send those emails that do not have their permissions, you can be accused of spamming.

Today, spamming is a serious offense especially in the world of information technology. Because the Internet is such a wild place, most authorities regard the privacy of each person as valuable and they continue to uphold this thinking even on the Internet.

With this, the creation of opt in list had gained tremendous acceptance. Because of its viability and feasibility to most online businesses, a lot of people have realized how important opt in lists are in email marketing.

Basically, opt in list refers to the list of email addresses of people who have agreed to subscribe to your mailing list. In this way, you can freely send emails that entail promotions, brochures, new product announcements, and every aspect of your marketing campaign.

When you build an opt in list, you do not only increase the probability of being successful in email marketing but also boost your sales and profits as well. This is because building an opt in list will give you the chance to stay in contact with your customers by getting their email address.

In this manner, you can continue to promote your products and services in which they are interested in because they have opted to subscribe in your mailing list. Hence, whatever it is that you feed them, chances are, they will most likely respond positively.

In reality, building an opt in list is actually letting the people realize the charisma and magic of email marketing. In this way, spams will be avoided, if not eliminated, and will not ruin the positive image of email marketing.

With spamming, email marketing becomes a disgraceful activity in the Internet. But with opt in list, online businesses can continue to boost their businesses through email marketing without having to worry about being accused of spamming.

In building opt in list, there are two types to be considered. The first one is the single opt-in and the other one is the double opt-in or the confirmed opt-in.

In building single opt-in list, online businesses would simply use a 'sign-up tag" in their web sites so that every time a person visits their website, he or she can opt to subscribe in the business" email list.

On the other hand, a confirmed opt-in list or double opt-in entails a confirmation message after the customer had subscribed to the particular web site's email list.

Usually, the confirmation takes place by replying on a system-generated message that asks for a confirmation of the subscription or by clicking on a link that entails the confirmation of the customer.

Whatever type of opt in list you would prefer, each has its own pros and cons when it comes to email marketing. But nevertheless, both are designed to give your online business the best solution possible in order to generate emails and permissions without having to get into trouble.

Indeed, email marketing is such a profitable business in the Internet. But it would not be complete and will never succeed without the help of the opt-in lists. These two must always go hand-in-hand in order to be successful in the virtual world of Internet marketing.

Chapter 15: The Essence of Internet Marketing Strategies to the Growth and Success of your Business

Supposedly you are one of the corporate executives of a large corporation. In a board of directors" meeting, it was discussed that the revenues as well as the volume of sales made during the previous month is comparatively lower compared to the revenues and volume of sales made several months ago. The decrease is more than what is expected, and present statistics show that the decreasing trend might continue due to uncontrollable market conditions. Once the problem is not addressed, the revenue of the corporation will suffer and it may even result to streamlining the corporate organization, which will affect most of the employees.

As a corporate executive, what can you contribute to solve the problem of the corporation where you belong? It is your responsibility to get the business back on track as well as ensuring the employees that they still have their work. At this point, what you need is to formulate effective marketing strategies that will address the problem of decreasing revenue and sales volume of your corporation.

Such marketing strategies will serve as the main foundation of your marketing plan. It must contain definition actions that will be implemented to address the problem of the corporation. For instance, you might use the strategy of offering low-cost yet high quality products or services to attract more consumers or convince potential clients to patronize your new product. By using such strategy, there is a high chance that you will be able to compensate previous losses and get the business on its profiting status.

In creating well-sound marketing strategies, you do not just build it without basis at all. In fact, such strategies must be integrated with your corporation's marketing objectives, policies, and tactics into a cohesive whole. Keep in mind that you are formulating marketing strategies to effectively carry out the corporation's mission of providing high-quality products or services at a lowest possible cost yet without sacrificing the profitability of the investment.

Marketing strategies are applicable in all types of investment, particularly on Internet marketing. Given the fact that the Internet is a marketplace with endless opportunities of creating your own niche and maximize any profit that you will earn from it, you need to have effective marketing strategies that will help you achieve your goal of earning more. Keep in mind that there are millions of websites that are competing for success in this lucrative investment. Your Internet marketing business must stay afloat amidst of this tight competition.

What are the Internet marketing strategies that will help you to get more potential customers, earning out of sales that you will make, and declare your Internet marketing career to be a successful one? Take a look on the following and learn how it will affect your Internet marketing business on a positive point of view.

• Begin with what you have. What are the possible edges of your product or your business as a whole compared to others? Does it stand out among other businesses with similar product? Being unique will help you get potential clients and eventually make your business a success. Nothing will beat your expertise of developing a product that will satisfy the needs of your target market.

• Bring your product and give it a unique image over the Internet. Use the power of words and images in expressing what you are really offering to the public. Make the description of your product as simple as possible yet straight to the point.

• One of the keys to Internet marketing success is the "click through" strategy where you will attract a customer to click on your ad and get through your product. The product that you will offer must be significant to the client looking for it, thus the use of online surveys will help you determine the products that are "in" and "out".

These are just some of the Internet marketing strategies that you can use in your business. There are still lots of strategies that you can use, but the aforementioned ones are the most basic. All complex strategies root from the basic, thus basic Internet marketing strategies are as effective as the complex ones.

Keep in mind the purpose of marketing—getting close or going beyond your return of investment within the least amount of time and the least financial spending possible. These Internet marketing strategies will help you achieve the purpose of marketing, as well as address any future problems that you may encounter along your Internet marketing projects.

Chapter 16: Know your Audience when Marketing Online

Internet marketing is quickly becoming one of the most popular advertising options available. The Internet reaches a worldwide audience and is available 24 hours a day. For this reason more and more potential customers are turning to the Internet for a variety of reasons including researching products and services and making purchases. As more and more consumers turn to the Internet for these reasons, it is important for businesses to establish an online presence. This is so important because failure to do so may result in their competitors gaining an edge over them in competing for sales. While it is important for business to begin Internet marketing campaigns it is also important for these same businesses to realize basic advertising principles still exist and they cannot neglect these principles. Most importantly those who advertise online have to be aware of who their target audience is and how to reach this audience.

As with any marketing campaign, business owners should do some market research before they launch their Internet marketing campaign. Ideally this will involve hiring a research consultant with a great deal of experience in conducting and evaluating this type of market research. The results of this research should determine the basic demographical information for the target audience. The results should also include information on how to reach this target audience. A business that cannot afford to hire a consultant to conduct this market research should still make an effort to obtain this information on their own. This can be done through informal polls of current clients. This information may not be as comprehensive as the information obtained in a more formal study but it can still provide a great deal of insight into the best way to reach the target audience. If you need help on this feel free to contact us via. http://www.qualitywebdesign.aaglobalsourcing.com/contact-quality-web-desig Your feedback is important to me.

Once this information is obtained, it is important to tailor the Internet marketing campaign to appeal to the target audience. There are a number of different variables which can be modified to ensure the right message is reaching the right people in a manner they can understand and in which they can relate. Some of the ways in which your Internet marketing campaign can be tailored in this way include the aesthetics of your website or advertisements, the wording of your copy and the use of more advanced design features such as audio and visual or interactive tools.

The aesthetic appeal of a website can greatly contribute to how the website is viewed by the members of the target audience. A website which is designed to attract the attention of an older generation with more conservative tastes should include muted colours, clean design and conservative graphics. This will help to ensure the target audience enjoys the website. Conversely if you are looking to appeal to a younger audience with more liberal viewpoints you might chose to design the website with bold colours, eye catching graphics and creative design features.

The copy you include on your website should also take your target audience into consideration. Consider the examples of a conservative and a liberal audience listed above to create a better understanding of how the copy on your website can appeal to the target audience. When marketing to a more conservative audience, the copy should be tailored to use formal language and use facts to back up viewpoints. However, when you are marketing to a more liberal audience or a younger audience you can consider using less formal language which is likely to appeal to the target audience. You can also focus more on emotion to express viewpoints.

Finally, when a website is created for the purposes of Internet marketing it is important for the design of the website to appeal to the target audience. You may wish to include audio and video clips on your website but these clips should appeal to the target audience. For example if your website sells skateboards you might consider incorporating audio clips from punk rock bands as opposed to country music bands. There may be some skateboarders who enjoy country music but in general punk rock music more closely represents the skating culture. Keeping these details in mind is very important for Internet marketing.

Chapter 17: Marketing your Business Online

If you are not already marketing your business online, it is time to start. Although there are a few exceptions, just about every business can benefit from online marketing. There are just so many advantages to this type of marketing. First of all, it is extremely affordable to market your business online. Other advantages to marketing your business online include the ability to reach a large target audience, the ability to reach potential customers all over the world and the ability to customize the marketing for different sectors of the target audience.

The affordability of Internet marketing is one of many reasons why many business owners are turning to the Internet for advertising. Advertising online is incredibly affordable especially when you consider how many potential customers a business owner can reach with an online marketing campaign. Most methods of online advertising are quite affordable and some of them do not have any direct costs. For example, you may choose to market your business online by participating in industry forums and posting links to your website whenever it is appropriate to do so. In this case the cost of creating and maintaining the website is insignificant in comparison to the number of potential clients you could reach through online marketing. Additionally, the costs associated with posting links to your website are incidental. You could consider the cost of having access to the

Internet as part of the cost but you most likely require Internet access for other reasons as well so it is completely worthwhile.

Reaching a large target audience is another very worthwhile reason for marketing your business online. You may have spent a great deal of time and energy doing market research and determine who your target audience is. You may have also spent a great deal of time trying to figure out the best way to reach this audience. This is a very sound marketing principle but as it applies to marketing on local television, radio and print media it only allows you to reach a limited audience. However, when you take your marketing to the Internet you automatically drastically increase your potential target audience because you now have the ability to reach members of your target audience around the world.

This ability to reach customers around the world is another major advantage to marketing your business online. Regardless of where you live and operate your business, you have the ability to reach those who have an interest in the products you sell or the services you provide no matter where they live. This makes it possible for you to do business with customers around the world.

Likewise the fact that the Internet is available 24 hours a day is also very beneficial to those who choose to market their products or services online. Shopping for products and services in person can be very difficult especially for individuals who work long hours or those who work unusual hours. These working conditions make it difficult for these individuals to do business and make purchases of products and services they need during regular business hours. However, business owners who have an online presence are much more convenient because unlike stores and calling centers, the website never closes. This convenience gives potential customers the ability to view products and services, compare these products and service to the ones offered by competitors and make a purchase at any hour of any day.

If you are a business owner or potential who is reading this book and you do not already have a strong online presence, you need to immediately start learning more about the world of Internet marketing. This is so important because if your competitors are marketing online, you may find they are gaining a steady advantage and are becoming more appealing to potential customers. Before too many of your potential customers become loyal customers of the competition it is time to start figuring out how you can market your business online and keep up with the competition. If you need help on this feel free to contact us via. http://www.qualitywebdesign.aaglobalsourcing.com/contact-quality-web-desig Your feedback is important to me.

Chapter 18: Internet Marketing: you need not to be a Computer Geek in Earning More through Online Business

Probably you are among those individuals who have daily nine-to-five jobs. Although provided with good compensation and a wide array of benefits, it is difficult to be just an ordinary employee. You need to be in the office before nine in the morning, or else a memorandum will be served to you, reminding that you are being "unpunctual" these recent days. After entering the office, you are now faced with the task of finishing all of the "paper works" (most of which are unnecessary) under time pressure and the pressure exerted to you by your boss. You will end the day with a lot of stress, thinking that you would want to quit and look for a job without such pressure in your shoulders.

But you have no choice. Nowadays, it is really difficult to find another job. There are individuals, despite of underemployment or low monthly salary, who accepts the job without hesitation. A single job vacancy is fought upon by a hundred applicants. Such scenario (which you probably experienced when you were still looking for your present job) will happen—if you will quit your present job.

Is there any alternative? Is there any chance that you will be able to escape the drudgery of your present job?

Fortunately, there is. And it is just right in front of a computer.

It is what we call Internet marketing—an online business opportunity that most online-based entrepreneurs loves.

Internet marketing is the most lucrative way of starting your home-based online business. It is the "big break" that many are looking for in a very long time. Do you want to become the boss? Do you want to work with your own time schedule? Do you want to work while wearing your favourite pajama and shirt? Do you want an extraordinary income that will exceed your expectation?

All of these are here; right in the heart of Internet marketing.

One of the common beliefs you will encounter in starting your home-based Internet marketing business is that you need to have the necessary technical expertise to succeed and continuously make a living with your online business. There are many individuals who believe that the lack of necessary knowledge and expertise about computer and Internet marketing prevents them from getting into the lucrative marketplace. They feel that they need to take first computer-related courses to get the job done.

However, it is a great marketing misconception

Contrary to this popular belief of becoming a computer geek first before earning money through Internet marketing, there are ways of ensuring success in online business without dealing too much with computer expertise. In fact, you do not have to be a web development guru or web programming expert to make your own living on the Internet.

There are Internet marketing business opportunities that are designed with simplicity. These opportunities have low barrier entries for individuals who lack technical know-how about the business. You can use these fully-automated systems to your advantage even if you are not a computer wizard. These programs are growing as your knowledge base expands.

What you need to learn are the basics of these automated systems (such as HTML and JavaScript codes) so that you can use them to your advantage. Most of successful Internet marketers studied this basic knowledge and apply what they have learned on simple automated systems. Only the fundamentals matter—and the rest will just follow.

Do not let the misconception prevent you from reaching your business objectives. Just because you did not go to a technical school and study computer programming-related courses means that you do not have the guts to be an Internet marketer for the rest of your life. Technical expertise is just a part of your success on Internet marketing—your own strategies and plans will do much of the work. The knowledge that you have (both on technical expertise and theoretical knowledge) will help you succeed on your Internet marketing career.

Becoming a computer geek is really amazing, yet its shine will lose if what he knows is only bounded by technical dimensions. Do not fret if you are not a computer geek or wizard. What matters most is what you can do to succeed in your Internet marketing career.

As simple as that, no questions asked! If you need help on this feel free to contact us via http://www.qualitywebdesign.aaglobalsourcing.com/contact-quality-web-desig Your feedback is important to me.

Chapter 19: Why Niche Marketing is the Way to go in succeeding Online

Niche Marketing is the last great frontier for the small business entrepreneur. Out there in the "real" world, small businesses do not have a half fair chance of competing against the giant international corporations of the world. The Internet has evened the odds for small business. The Internet has created a real equal opportunity for those who are willing to use it. There are several different ways to make use of niche marketing and succeed. All of the ways require getting a domain and a webhost, building web pages and adding content. Those are just the basic basics of Internet Marketing in any form. Then there are the choices of how to go about building a successful niche marketing site that will provide you with a profit....hopefully a very large profit.

1. You can create an informational product. An informational product can be articles, reports, columns, audio or video, or other things. These can be sold as standalone products or used for advertisement or promotional causes.

2. You can build a content rich web site that will be so interesting it will draw potential customers again and again.

3. You can publish newsletters and ezines that are so full of pertinent information that people will happily

pay for subscriptions to them.

All of the above listed ways can be used to create a niche marketing website that has the capacity to make money. There are two things that all of these methods have in common.

1. The topic must be one that helps people solve a problem, makes them healthier or happier, or provides them with information that they want or need in some way.

2. The content of the website, no matter the topic, must be relevant, timely and interesting to the people who are reading it and the website must be easily navigated.

Chapter 20: Using Online Courses for Internet Marketing

Online courses, or email courses are becoming an increasingly popular way for savvy Internet marketers to promote their products and services. Online courses or email courses essentially include short online presentations or emails which include insightful information on a particular niche subject. These courses are usually offered in multiple, short segments to keep the students interested in the topic. This type of advertising serves a useful purpose and many of the participants do not even realize they are being subjected to a marketing campaign. This book will discuss creating and distributing an online or email course for the purposes of advertising your business.

The creation of an online course of an email course should begin with a solid idea for a series of educational articles which pertain to your business and will be of interest to your potential customers. Educational email courses can sometimes be sold for profit themselves but if you are interested in using the courses as marketing tools you will most likely be offering these courses free of charge in an effort to entice potential customers to purchase your products or services.

Determining the topic of your courses is very important because it can dictate the success of your marketing effort. Consider an online retailer of running shoes. This business owner may want to develop a series of email courses on subjects such as training for a marathon, preventing injuries, increasing speed and running for fun. Each of these courses may contain a few segments which offer different perspectives on the subject. These courses are ideal for this business because they are subjects which are likely to be of interest to the customers of the business. Likewise a real estate agent may opt to offer email courses on subjects such as understanding mortgage options, finding a lender or house hunting. Again these are all subjects which are likely to be of interest to the real estate agents clients.

The distribution list for your online or email courses should mostly include members of your target audience. This can be achieved by either offering the course as a download online where only interested Internet users will partake in the course or only emailing the course to recipients who have specifically expressed an interest in receiving more information about your products and services and have submitted their email address for this purpose.

Once you decide on a subject for your online or email course, seek out a qualified writer to create the content for your online or email course. This will help to give your copy a more professional appearance. The writer can assist you by creating copy which is informative and useful to your readers but is also well written, clear, concise and easy to understand. If your niche topic is highly specialized you might have to provide the writer with product information as well as research materials to ensure the content is informative and accurate. Additionally, you should review the content once it is completed to verify the accuracy.

When distributing your email course or launching your online course, it is helpful to request feedback from the users as the conclusion of the course. This is completely voluntary but when users respond they can provide you with useful feedback which will be extremely helpful if you intend to launch a similar marketing campaign in the future.

Chapter 21: Internet Marketing Service - Just how important it is to your Online Business Career

Online credit card application and approval.

Google AdSense.

Online payments through credit card transactions.

These are just some of the innovations integrated on the famous Information Superhighway—the Internet. It paved the way to the creation of one of the most lucrative business—the Internet marketing.

Internet marketing is just similar to traditional marketing wherein your primary goal is to promote and sell whatever products or services you have to offer for sale effectively. The only difference is that Internet marketing is using the Internet to achieve your business goal. Unlike in traditional marketing wherein you need to establish your business in a "physical market", Internet marketing revolves on the concept of online selling, that is, the acquisition of goods and services through automated system.

In other words, you do not need an actual shop to display your products for sale. You don't need to hire additional employees who will help you run your business. You can manage your online business without any actual shop or additional employees. All you need to have is a website that will serve as your 'shop" where your visitors and clients can see your products and/or services for sale. The success of your business will largely depend on your website as well as the strategies that you will use to manage your Internet marketing business.

There was an Internet marketer who shared some of his expertise on Internet marketing. According to him, a website must address five specific aspects of Internet marketing in order to succeed.

These are as follows:
1. Getting people to visit your website.
2. Getting people to stay at your website.
3. Getting people to visit your website again.
4. Getting people to have transactions with you at your website
5. Getting people to have repeated or multiple transactions at your website.

From these five specific aspects, you may conclude that Internet marketing is about getting people into your website and do transactions with you. Keep in mind that you will not be able to earn revenues from your Internet marketing business if your website (which serves as your shop) cannot convert its visitors into loyal customers. Thus, your business objective now is to get more people to visit your website and possibly persuade them to make purchases of anything that you offer for sale.

This is where Internet marketing services comes into action. Such service, together with your marketing strategies, will help you get a majority of the Internet traffic to go to your site and convert them not just into sure but also into "repeat" buyers.

Just how important Internet marketing service is to your online business? Consider the following instances and learn how Internet marketing service affects almost every aspect of your Internet marketing career:

1. At the earlier part of your online business, you are required to have your own website. As mentioned earlier, your site must attract people that could be your potential clients. Thus, you need to avail of different Internet marketing services that will help you make your site as attractive as possible to the Internet public, such as website design and development, content building, search engine optimization, keyword research, and others.

2. Part of your Internet marketing business is advertising. You need to promote your products and/or services effectively so that you will be able to get more people who will make transactions with you. Services that are associated with advertising your online business include newsletter, e-mail marketing, online press releases, mailing lists, article marketing, affiliate marketing, and others.

3. There is no single Internet marketer who succeeds without partners on his side. Thus, you need to get the services of your online partners (ad serving firms, professional marketing strategists, and others) who are

willing to lend you a hand in achieving your online business goals.

All of existing Internet marketing services serves a common ground to all online entrepreneurs—that is, to ensure that Internet marketing industry exists continuously, thus giving everybody the opportunity of earning online. Without this Internet marketing services, the existence of this lucrative industry will probably cease, the dream of a five- to seven-digit revenue will remain to be a dream forever.

If you have plans of getting involved on Internet marketing, be sure that you are aware of the services and keep your online business alive and kicking.

Chapter 22: Internet Marketing Services - the Oxygen of your Online Career

Internet marketing is the innovation that successful online-based entrepreneurs will be thankful to for the rest of their lives. Before this, many websites were at the brink of bankruptcy because they could not properly promote their sites and were finding it hard to find clients and customers. Low sales are generated everyday, or worse, no sales at all. Cash outflow is greater than cash inflow, and the net is almost in its negative status. They advertise here and there, reprinting sales copy and distributing it to different places, and hiring financial advisers to handle the financial management of their investment. Despite of their determination to uplift their business and maintain its profitability, their investment is always at the risk of losing all of what they have worked for.

Upon the intervention of Internet on their business, the conduct of their business suddenly shifted on its advantageous point. Operational costs have been cut down by more than half of its original cost, got more clients than what they have expected, and generated additional revenues through different online-based earning opportunities. The way their products are sold now have been taking a different approach. Even if they do not personally meet their client, the customer is willing to pay for the product or service provided.

Suddenly, the Internet radically changed the fate of many businessmen. Nowadays, they have the courage of starting more Internet marketing business and earn more through these opportunities.

Internet marketing is looked upon by online entrepreneurs and marketing experts as a well-established concept and an important tool in expanding their market within the shortest time possible. It includes the concept of redefining business and product offerings, higher ROI (return of investment), branding products, and a different marketing approach.

Thus, it is important for aspiring Internet marketers to learn the concepts behind Internet marketing in order for them to succeed in their online career. A strong Internet marketing foundation will help them formulate their own avenue of maximizing their revenues from their online business.

Aside from such concepts, another thing that must be learned by an Internet marketer is the nature of existing Internet marketing services. It is important that they understand the existing services to maximize its capability in improving their online business. It is among their basic knowledge to become successful on Internet marketing.

What are the basic Internet marketing services? It is imperative that we understand the nature of each service.
1. Website marketing- creating a website is not a simple task. Your website must be profitable

enough to sustain the needs of your business. Expect tight competition among other Internet marketers who also want to grab a slice of this lucrative business opportunity.

2. Website promotion- this service includes a web design that is according to your personal preferences and the nature of your online business, the logo design of your online-based company, multimedia features, media campaign for increased site visibility over the Internet, creation of customer interface, and search engine optimization.

3. Promotion of website through online advertising schemes such as affiliate marketing programs and ad serving technology, which is commonly administered by search engines and high-traffic websites. It commonly includes search engine marketing, copywriting, creation of sales copies, keyword selection, periodical reviewing, and newsletter creation.

4. Web analytic services- it includes service performance optimization that is client-focused, reducing online operational costs, increased revenue generation, and assessment of the lifetime value of each client.

These services will help you ensure that you will have a slim chance of losing your online investment. These are provided by different Internet marketing experts as well as marketing specialists who are willing to help you upgrade marketing tools that you have and change your existing marketing strategies according to the present needs of your online business.

Remember that you will not exist for long on the Internet marketing arena if you will not use the aforementioned services. It will serve as the "oxygen" of your business. Do not consider such services to be just a simple aid for your business growth, but consider this as one of the integral components of your investment. Without them, your Internet marketing career will be at the brink of failure.

Internet marketing services is vital to the development and continuity of your online business. Make sure that you use these services wisely and you will soon see your profits grow.

Chapter 23: Quality Web Design - becoming a Proficient Online Marketer

The Internet marketing business is a booming industry. Individuals who have started from scratch became among the successful Internet marketers who capitalized on their Internet-connected personal computer unit, basic knowledge on Internet marketing, wildest imagination, creativity, and some self-confidence just to earn the money that they want. They are not afraid of the possible losses they might incur along their Internet marketing career. All they have in mind is just there is always a tomorrow that will give them the chance to fulfill their goals they have missed the previous days.

Fortunately, they did it.

Because of their hard work and determination in earning through Internet marketing business, the industry has flourished rapidly due to the increased offerings of various products and services for lower prices. Aside from the increased volume of online shoppers over the Internet, the industry opened its doors for aspiring Internet marketers to grab a huge slice of the luxurious Internet marketing business. With several noted benefits such as 24/7 availability, international coverage, and low start-up costs, Internet marketing became the key to business growth not just on a consistent but also on an exponential basis. Just imagine generating £40,000 last month and jumping to £50,000 this month.

Despite of the opportunity of earning huge amounts of money from Internet marketing, there are still online entrepreneurs who do not have the capability and sufficient knowledge of making their sites sell to the public, mainly because of the very stiff competition rocking the Internet-based marketing industry. Even the site that is designed carefully with a shopping cart and inventory listing facilities, if it is not generating web traffic, the site can be considered as a total failure so as the effort of the website owner to earn on Internet marketing.

At this point, the services of an Quality Web Design must be an important factor to consider. In exchange for a corresponding fee, they will help you increase web traffic to your websites, thus increasing your chances of earning more. Such Internet marketing company can do it in several ways such as affiliate marketing programs, pay-per-click (PPC) advertising schemes, and search engine optimization (SEO). Although you are relatively familiar with these marketing concepts, you still lack time and expertise to perfect the concept. The Quality Web Design, through their consultants and technical people, will be the one to apply the necessary strategies for your site to build necessary traffic and increase generated sales along the process.

The core of Quality Web Design business is dependent on your efforts and skills. As a matter of fact, if your online-based business is service-oriented, the start-up costs in setting it up is relatively low since it does not require inventories at all. However, you need to have the necessary knowledge, skills, and expertise on Internet marketing before you can start your business. These factors are commonly provided from self-study, attending actual or webinars (seminars over the Web), or getting a mentor from Quality Web Design who will guide you along the course. The start-up costs on acquiring necessary knowledge may vary, depending on the type of education you have obtained. Other costs may revolve on several factors such as server maintenance and support as well as website design and development.

This will also include building a concrete business plan that will indicate the potential growth of your online-based business. Aside from using it is the main guide of your Internet marketing business, you can also use it to obtain necessary funding for your business either from venture capitalists or commercial lenders.

The cost of hiring the services of an Quality Web Design will also depend on its advertising efforts, the source of the Internet traffic, and the keywords of the site that needs to be optimized. It is because of the fact that website-based keywords require more work from Quality Web Design people to produce expected results. Areas of concerns such as mode of advertising, present marketing strategies, as well other factors are also some of the expertise provided by Quality Web Design.

There are some companies that charge their clients

based on the increase on sales generated by the implementation of their own strategies. It may be in the form of a percentage of increased sales from your site over a certain period of time.

Although it is quite expensive to hire the services of an Quality Web Design, you will be able to see the results to be better than handling the business all by yourself, especially if you are just a novice on Internet marketing. The hundreds of dollars/pounds you may spend from hiring Quality Web Design is nothing compared to the thousands of dollars/pounds you will generate every month—not counting the increase on sales.

Chapter 24: Internet Marketing Promotion and Advertising: Build a Successful Online Career

Internet marketing is surrounded by facts that every aspiring online entrepreneur should know. Although you have heard several success stories about individuals who succeeded and earned thousands to millions of dollars/pounds through Internet marketing, they are also bounded by these facts existing around the industry.

First, just like the typical business investment, you cannot make a fortune overnight on Internet marketing. Successful Internet marketers have spent several years to perfect their marketing strategies. They have started from studying the "ins and outs" of the business opportunity, applied existing strategies, formulated their own marketing strategies, and test their new strategies to their marketing business. Although Internet marketing offers a lucrative business opportunity for everyone, it takes some time before you could earn millions of dollars through Internet marketing. You will start from several hundreds and after several months or years, you will be able to earn thousands of dollars on Internet marketing revenues.

Second, your competitors will always be your competitors. There are instances wherein they will use you for their advantage. Of course, we do not want to ruin friendships here, but it is a fact that you must be careful of. You can work hand in hand with other Internet marketers, but you must ensure that you are not working with "hungry predators" or those who will not use your generosity for their advantage of earning more money.

Lastly, getting potential clients is the hardest part of your Internet marketing career. Remember that the success of your Internet marketing business will depend on how you will attract potential clients coming from the majority of traffic around the Internet. Even if you have a well-designed website with useful facilities such as information catalogue and shopping cart services, once you failed to attract large web traffic towards your site, your Internet marketing business will be of total failure.

Among the aforementioned facts, the last one is what you need think of most. As previously mentioned, the success of your Internet marketing career depends on how you build your clientele base. Such clientele base will serve as your "bloodline" that will keep your marketing career alive. Without them, the Internet marketing industry will remain to be a dream for individuals who want to earn more money.

If you want to attract potential clients and convert them into loyal product evangelizers, you must learn the whereabouts of Internet marketing promotion and advertising. Promoting and advertising your Internet marketing is crucial to your website and to your career as well. Through these strategies, you will be able to attract motivated people who are willing to purchase whatever you are offering. Taking time to create some buzz about your website will keep them coming back and create an intriguing impression to those individuals who have not got a try of your products or services.

Promotion and advertising will help you get the targeted traffic that you want in the early run of your Internet marketing career. In fact, the cost of promoting and advertising your site on the Internet is not as expensive as advertising your products and services through conventional methods such as billboards and classified ads of different newspapers. Even if you do not have that large marketing budget, you can still promote and advertise your site using various alternative and low-cost promotional methods.

So what are the characteristics of a good Internet marketing promotion and advertising? Take a look on the following items and make sure that your promotion and advertising tools possess these characteristics:

• It must have a long-lasting effect. Do not just use an advertising medium once and discard it. Find ways on how you will be able to use it for several times. You may use a similar approach on each advertising tool and create customer familiarity with the advertising tool as well as the product or service you are advertising. Think of several successful promotions and advertisement such as for Energizer batteries and others.
• An effective Internet marketing promotion and advertising have variations. Do not just stick with a

single ad format. Change the colour, text, and the message of your advertisements but do not alter its feature character. The alterations must be done in the consideration of a long-lasting ad effect.

Do not be afraid to explore new options. If you think these new ideas will help you promote and advertise your Internet marketing business effectively, then do it. The more you broaden your promotion and advertising efforts, you will be able to succeed in your Internet marketing business career.

Chapter 25: Quality Web Design towards your Online Business Career Success

Everyone needs a mentor. If you want to be successful in your chosen university degree, you need to be under the care of your university professors who have the necessary knowledge and expertise in your chosen university degree. They will prepare you to the real world and equip you with the necessary knowledge and expertise so that you will be able to be successful and stand against any obstacles that will block your way towards reaching your goals, whatever it is.

Even starting Internet marketers needs to be educated by Internet marketing experts. Keep in mind that vital factors are on risk in this type of investment - your name, reputation, effort, and most especially your monetary investment. Once you have plunged in Internet marketing without learning first the necessary knowledge and strategies, expect that it will be the cause of the downfall of your Internet marketing career. Thus, to avoid losing what you already have, you need somebody to guide you throughout your Internet marketing career.

Quality Web Design is here to help you

Quality Web Design was founded in 2010 by the Internet marketing expert Ade Asefeso that is focused on the research, development, and test of cost-efficient e-business and e-commerce marketing strategies and automated solutions that could be applied to small and home-based business owners and produce revenues and profits. As one of the recognized leader in the Internet marketing industry, Quality Web Design continues to develop practical and cost-efficient marketing strategies for online and offline-based businesses of all size. Because of their innovative solutions and effective marketing recommendations, their websites draw more than 5,000 web visitors every month.

How can Quality Web Design help you with your Internet marketing career? There are several steps that you need to undergo with them so that you will be able to achieve success in your chosen business opportunity.

1. Choosing a Product- you will be provided with a wide selection of products or services that you can endorse over the Internet. They will also provide you the list of products and services that are most purchased over online shopping websites.

2. Getting Started with a Website- Internet marketing will be of no use to you if you do not have a website to start with. You will learn how to start with your Internet marketing website, such as its design and development, web page optimization, registering under a unique and original domain name, and others. You will also know what are the 'do's and don'ts" in creating and developing a website.

3. Writing Sales Copy- sales copy is essential to

Internet marketing, since it will serve as your "campaign material' in endorsing your products or services. You will learn about the appropriate contents of your sales copy and how you will effectively market it to potential clients.

4. Getting Internet Traffic- you will not succeed on your Internet marketing career if you do not have Internet traffic to convert into loyal product evangelists. You will learn much about the promotional tools that are used and proven effective in marketing your site and its products or services.

5. Search Engines- this will bring you the targeted Internet traffic that you want towards your website. You will learn several search engine factors that have direct effects on your website, such as keywords, optimized web pages, search engine spider, unique niches, and others.

6. Starting a Newsletter- by getting subscribers to read newsletters, you will be able to build a strong clientele base. Feeding them with latest and consistently updated information will help you get the targeted traffic that you want.

7. Testing Email Marketing Solutions- emails are now widely used by Internet marketers in advertising their products and getting the clients that they need. You will learn how you will convert your regular email into traffic-generating machines as well as the things that you need and need not to include in sending emails to your subscribers.

8. Recruiting Affiliates- you are not alone. There are thousands of Internet marketers out there and getting them as affiliates will surely boost your Internet marketing business. You will learn how to recruit affiliates once you have established your Internet marketing company.

There are hundreds to thousands of success stories about online marketers who sought the help of Quality Web Design. Want to have your own success story? Try Quality Web Design and see the difference!

Chapter 26: Get Home-based Internet Marketing Business its Celebrity Status through Effective Online Promotion

It feels good to be an ordinary employee as long as you are well-compensated and you receive privileges and benefits that are entitled to you. Good for you if you have alternate jobs after office hours or during weekends wherein you will be able to generate additional income to finance you and your family's important expenditures.

However, there are instances wherein you come to think that the income you receive both from your regular and alternate work is still insufficient to compensate your expenditures given the fact that the prices of basic commodities and other necessities are consistently increasing. There is no chance that your salary will also increase every time the prices of basic commodities also increase. It is your responsibility to sustain the needs of your family.

During those instances, there are employees who are brave enough to face the risk of getting into business. Thus, they retire from their previous work, collect the necessary cash benefits due to them, and use this as their starting capital for their business venture. Most of them get into home-based business wherein they start selling several merchandises to their neighbours and later selling such items to the business district within their locality.

There are also employees who realized that establishing a home-based business is still incapable of sustaining the needs of their respective families. It still requires hundreds to thousands of dollars of capital and they need to work on a double effort so that they can sustain the needs of their home-based business. With regards to selling home-based products to the business district within their locality, they stressed that it needs additional capital and several employees who will handle the business outside your residence.

That is why these employees are getting involved into home-based Internet marketing business. They clear some space inside their house that will serve as their "business office" (they also makes use of their bedrooms as offices) and purchase a single personal computer unit that is connected on the Internet. What they typically do is to surf on the Internet, research for several Internet-based earning opportunities that does not require huge starting capital, and learning the strategies needed to succeed in this type of investment.

Home-based Internet marketing business is advantageous for individuals who start with minimal capital input. There are also various Internet-based marketing programs that do not require you to purchase products and sell it to interested individuals over the net. For instance, there is the affiliate marketing program where you need to have your own site registered in your own domain name as the "affiliate" for the program. What you have to do is to advertise the assigned merchant's website to your own site and you will earn several dollars for every click that will be generated by the affiliate merchant site's URL placed in your own website.

One of the secrets of skyrocketing revenues generated from home-based Internet marketing business is the promotion that you employ. You need to let the world know that you have a website where they can find interesting stuffs and useful information and they need to click on different online advertisements placed into your site to access such useful information. The success of every Internet-based business is vital especially in terms of promoting it to the Internet community.

What are the effective promotions available for your home-based Internet marketing business? Take a sneak peek on the following and determine what kind of promotion is best suited for your business.

1. Search engine. This is one of the ways of getting your website popular to Internet users. Your site must appear on the top pages of every search engine results made by Internet users. Without your site on the top pages of search engine page results, it is hard for you to attract potential clients to visit your website.

2. Online advertising. This is one of the best methods of getting your website popular to Internet users. All you have to do is contact online-based advertising companies and let them do the job of advertising your site for a corresponding fee. Of

course, it is relatively cheaper compared on advertising your home-based business outside the Internet community.

3. Article directories. If you are looking for some "free promotions", then this is for you. You just need to write articles about the contents of your site and submit it to article directories. You will be required to include a brief description about yourself as the author and the URL of your website. This is one of the effective marketing strategies used in online-based businesses. If you need help on this feel free to contact us via. http://www.qualitywebdesign.aaglobalsourcing.com/ contact-quality-web-desig Your feedback is important to me.

It feels good when you are earning without spending too much money and exerting too much effort. However, you need to determine the best promotion tool for your home-based Internet marketing business so that you will be able to achieve success despite of the risks involved.

Chapter 27: Internet Marketing Firm: Lending a Hand of Success to Online Marketers

The world of employment is similar to a rat race where all job hunters are in pursuit of a single cheese, in which case is the job that they are looking for. There is a stiff competition between job hunters, carrying all their best arsenals (their credentials and achievements) to best other candidates for the job. With a few vacant jobs available against hundreds of thousands of jobless individuals, it is really difficult to score the position without undergoing extensive screening from prospective employers.

Beyond the limelight of employment, there exist an opportunity for everyone to make hundreds to thousands of dollars/pounds each month without experiencing the hassle of being under work pressure. The salary in this opportunity is not fixed; meaning, there is always a room for increase or decrease, depending on the ability of the individual who will have a try on it. Moreover, this income-generating opportunity can be done within the comfort of your home, thus lessening the stress yet increasing the time to be with your family anytime of the day, any day of the week.

This is the power of Internet marketing—letting everybody aware that earning is not just within the portals of a corporate organization. You take charge of your own corporate organization. You are just like

101

a one-man army, eliminating rebels and enemies even without a platoon or battalion that will support through your mission.

More and more individuals are getting started with their chosen Internet marketing business opportunity simply because they have already realized the benefits of starting one within the comfort of their home. Even in a makeshift office, they can earn as much as what is earned by a corporate executive, even much larger than that. With these benefits aligned for those individuals who have the courage to take the challenge as well as the risks involved on Internet marketing business, many aspiring online marketers are getting the rope and try their luck as well as their clever minds in formulating the marketing strategies needed with this unique career.

You have heard success stories about Internet marketers who have already build a marketing empire by just starting with a single website or two. They have invested sufficient time and expertise in mastering the skills and art of Internet marketing, thus resulting on their inevitable success. However, they also became novices, constantly wondering what must be done and what must take place. At this point wherein they do not know what to do, they have done one single step that they did not regret doing during their entire Internet marketing career.

And that is hiring the services of an Internet marketing firm.

Such Internet marketing firm is dedicated on helping

novice and even long-time Internet marketers to achieve the market share that they want, profit they expect, and the customer loyalty that they are longing for through effective Internet-based marketing strategies and system. In addition, these Internet marketing firms are not working alone. They are working with several marketing partners that have their respective areas of expertise. In fact, Internet marketing firms have a prominent portfolio of clients that ranging from small and medium-sized organizations to Internet-based Fortune 100 corporations. Internet marketing firms are composed of qualified, experienced, and professional Internet marketing consultants and experts not just from United States and UK but from different countries as well.

These firms are not just ordinary marketing firms, since the success on Internet marketing firms are largely dependent on the ability of the marketer to determine the best opportunity that will help him reach his target clients in a cost-efficient manner. Thus, they are not just concentrating on the theoretical aspects of Internet marketing but they are also engage in the implementation of customized web systems as well as integrated online marketing solutions that concentrate on client base development, customer retention, and brand awareness.

Aside from those aforementioned services, Internet marketing firms are also aware of the needs of web customers, particularly those who are frequently using search engines to find relative contents that they want. Thus, search engine marketing is one of the firm's expertises to attract more visitors on the client's website. Their search engine marketing services are designed to get every website visible to potential buyers over the Internet.

Internet marketing firm is indeed of great help in grabbing the slice of the lucrative business of Internet marketing.

Chapter 28: Internet Marketing Professionals - how to Earn Respect from the Online Community

Engineers, doctors, nurses, accountants, and lawyers.

They are what we call as professionals. They are individuals with recognized knowledge and expertise on a certain field of endeavour. They are entitled by law and existing policies to practice their respective professions. They are worthy of the standards of their profession, giving them legal licenses to practice their respective professions. Thus, they are the "authorities" in their respective field of endeavours.

Along with their tag as professionals, these individuals are bounded by proper etiquette with regards to their actions and behaviours. As professionals, they are expected to deliver required services to the public and at the same time deal with other individuals and professionals in an appropriate manner. They are looked upon as leaders; thus they are expected to act as real professionals when dealing with their work and other people.

Professionals are everywhere—in various construction sites, real estate markets, hospitals, county courts, and other places. Even the Internet marketing industry is surrounded by various professionals—Internet business consultants, web content writers, software developers, web designers, and others.

Thus, the Internet marketing is a pool of web-based professionals who are working not just for their personal interest but for the development of the industry as well. But what does it take to be considered as one of the Internet marketing professionals?

As previously mentioned, the definition of a professional revolves around the concept of "an individual who has recognized knowledge and expertise on a certain field of endeavour". As a professional, you are considered to be worthy of the standards of your profession. You need to show to the world that you are really worth to be considered as a professional through creating a professional image.

However, building a professional image is not as easy as you think. In fact, it entails a great deal of time and effort. Your knowledge and expertise is not just the working factor here. You must also consider the conduct of your business in a professional manner, especially on the Internet where you are dealing with clients whom you do not know and you do not see.

Now, how will you start building your professional image? Consider the following aspects in creating your image on the Internet marketing industry.

• Your attitude is among the most essential aspects in creating your professional image on the Internet. It can either make you or kill your career in an instant. The manner you deal with your fellow Internet marketers, clients, and the concerns they want you to answer such as questions, comments, and compliments will reflect on your professionalism as a reputable Internet marketer.

1. Courtesy is also an important factor. As previously mentioned, you are dealing with people whom you are not seeing and you do not know. Despite of that gap, make your "unseen" clients feel that they are very much appreciated. You must be respectful and warm in accommodating their queries and concern. Even in words, always express your gratitude to them.

2. Honesty is the best policy. Do not mislead your web-based clients or else you will lose them. Remember that you have to earn their trust for you to build long-term relationships with them.

3. When dealing with your clients, always go above and beyond their expectations. Always listen to the concerns of your clients. As a professional, you are expected to hear from your clients even if you know and understand most of the aspects of your Internet marketing business.

4. Unsatisfied clients always complain about poor technical support. You need to make yourself personally available to assist your

clients with their needs. If possible, respond to their emails and return their call as fast as possible.

5. Although it is a loss if you will refund the money of unsatisfied clients, you need to. Do not argue with the issue or blast nasty things unto them. Always be apologetic, courteous, and know why they are unsatisfied. Remember the rule that "customers are always right", even if you feel that they are wrong.

6. Your website is the reflection of yourself and your Internet marketing business. It must be professional-looking, complete with product and contact information, and easy ordering protocol.

7. Be respectful to your fellow Internet marketers. Keep in mind that you must build a friendly competition on the business and not on personal preferences.

Internet marketing professionals possess those aforementioned aspects. Thus, before getting respect from the Internet community, show to them that you are worthy of their respect and build a professional image on the Internet.

Chapter 29: How to Make your Online Advertising Business Produce Money on Internet Marketing

The success or failure of your Internet marketing business depends largely on the Internet users. If they are interested on the products and services that you are offering for sale, definitely you can expect hundreds to thousands of dollars/pounds in revenues from your online business. On the other hand, if they are just too lazy to hear what you want to say and what you are offering, better shut down your personal computer unit and find some other ways of earning money.

As an Internet marketer, you do not want the second scenario to happen to your Internet marketing career. To be the "exception to the rule", you must attract more web visitors to your site and turn them into long-term clients and build a loyal clientele base. Once you have satisfied such requirements, expect that there is something in return—positive returns, to be specific.

How will you say to Internet users that you need them to keep your online business alive? In fact, you need not to tell them straight to the point that you badly need them. All you need is a clever mind and some online advertising to get them without making them realize that you badly need them.

There are various online advertising methods on the Internet and each method has their product that works better on specific industries. There are huge numbers of individuals and companies operating online who wants to advertise what they have to offer, and there are also huge numbers of individuals and companies on the Internet who are willing to provide some advertising spaces. However, considering that the online advertising market is quite large, it will be inefficient for the advertisers as well as the providers of these online advertising spaces to individually meet and talk about the terms of conditions of advertising.

The individual or company who wish to advertise will certainly contact an online-based advertising company that are willing to provide the space that the advertiser needs as well as distribute their advertisements to different venues on the Internet at the same time.

The more benefits are now towards the online advertising firm. And you are considering an online advertising business.

But before you go, there are several things you need to consider first.

Start to gather a collection of websites or online companies that are willing to place advertisements on their sites. Select sites that are getting high web traffic every month. Once you have gathered advertising site venues, you may now start soliciting advertising clients. These advertisers will pay a certain amount of money that will commensurate with the exposure of their products or services on your advertising site venues. For instance, if you have contracted with 20 websites that are receiving an average of 200,000 web visitors every month, you can sell as much as 2,000,000 advertising exposures every month on each advertiser. In case that you have negotiated around 20 advertising venues on each website, you can sell an equivalent of 20 advertising clients with 2,000,000 advertising exposures every month. If an advertiser only pays for 1,000,000 advertising exposures, you can still sell the remaining 1,000,000 advertising exposures for a total of 11 advertising clients.

Now, what are the types of online advertising that you can offer? Here are some of the offerings that you can sell to individuals or companies who wish to advertise their products or services on the Internet.

1. Banner ads- these ads are typically pictorial ads that are commonly viewed on high-traffic sites and includes a hyperlink back to the advertiser's own site. These are priced according to the number of ads shown. For instance, banner ads can be sold in lots of 250,000 impressions each.
2. Sponsorship ads- these ads are commonly larger than banner ads, which sometimes contain considerable amount of text. These are typically placed on high-traffic areas such as ezines or online newsletters. It is priced according to the number of readers of the newsletter or publication in which the ad is placed.

3. Pay per click (PPC) ads- these ads are priced according to the number of clicks generated through site visitors, These are commonly text ads, though there are PPC ads that are pictorial-based.

Starting your own online advertising business is another opportunity of earning more money on the Internet marketing industry.

Chapter 30: The Best Marketing and Delivery System for your Online Video Products

In the past year it has become easier than ever to launch an online video business-or even start your own niche TV channel. Brightcove.com is the best package available for marketing and selling your online video products. This site provides Internet publishing services, which means that you can create your own Internet channel on Brightcove.

Brightcove includes everything you need to sell video content to your customers: digital rights management support, payment processing, download and delivery, and customer service support. You set rental and sale prices for your video downloads. (You can rent video downloads for one, three, seven, or thirty days.) Brightcove lets you launch an Internet video channel on your own web site and grow your channel into a thriving online video or TV business. Brightcove also lets you grow your business through syndication to affiliate web sites. This is Internet video at its best.

What makes this site so special is the Brightcove business model. Members can select one of various revenue streams and control where their content appears on the Internet. One revenue option is to allow Brightcove to add their advertising to your video-when this happens, they split advertising revenue with you. (No ads are run on paid video downloads.) Brightcove gives producers control over how ads appear in their videos. A company can even choose to host its content on the Brightcove platform and set its own rates for advertising.

The Brightcove Platform for professional content providers and marketers allows you to set up video channels on your own web site and syndicate your video content to affiliate sites. As your audience increases, your revenue from sales and advertising will also increase.

A free Brightcove Network account gives you unlimited access to video broadcasting, storage, delivery, and distribution services. As soon as you register, you can start publishing your videos and set up your Internet channel. The best thing about Brightcove is how it empowers users. You used to be a creator of video products for the Worldwide Web-Brightcove gives you the power to be a broadcaster of online video products.   Concentrate on what you do best One of the most powerful aspects of the Brightcove Platform is how you can use it to create a community of users around your site. Brightcove lets you create what is essentially your own YouTube niche site. You can encourage viewers to put their own videos on your site, just like users do on YouTube. You control all aspects of this process, of course-review, approval, and publishing of videos uploaded by your viewers.

The greatest benefit of Brightcove is that it lets you concentrate on what you do best-creation and marketing of video products. This is astonishing; it is now possible to launch an Internet TV channel without the huge capital investment traditionally required for putting a show on the air. Brightcove is a platform that can scale to handle whatever you give it, and it is already hosting content from some of the largest media companies in the world.

Chapter 31: Using Facebook as an Online Marketing Tool

Social networking websites are becoming more and more popular each day. Websites like these are primarily used as a social utility that will enable people to connect with other people. With Facebook, you will be able to connect with friends, acquaintances, and with other people who you study and live with.

One social networking website that is very popular among many people today is Facebook. With Facebook, you will be able to get your very own profile page where you can upload an unlimited amount of photos, share videos, and also a place where you will let people viewing a little about you.

Although this is a great social networking site that will enable you to keep in touch with your friends and acquaintances as well as meet new people and make new friends, it is also a website that made a lot of internet marketers drool.

With over 110 million active subscribers and still continuing to grow, you know that this place is the place to market.

If you own a business and you are reaching for an 18 to 25 demographic to sell your products, you will see that Facebook will be able to provide you with your target customers. Most subscribers here are aged between 18 and 25, which is called the 'tech-savvy youth audiences".

With Facebook, you will not only target your ads on specific regions and universities, but you will also be able to get your fair share of audience. Here, you will see that when you join, you will be able to readily use tools that can really help you advertise your products and services.

You can customize your profile in order to make it unique and attract your target audience and you can also post blogs and even syndicate your blog page using RSS. If you have video ads about your products or services, you can post it here on Facebook as well.

When you register with Facebook, you can also add friends. Try adding as much as you can and establish some relationship. If you already know someone who uses Facebook, add them and try to get them to promote the products or services you offer.

This is one great feature of Facebook. With it, you will be able to get people who are connected to your network to advertise for you. This way, you will see that you will be able to market your product more effectively by getting people in other network know about your products or services.

Another great tool that you can use in Facebook is the ability to let you add applications in your profile page. Here, you will be able to add games and other applications in your profile page, which can be great in attracting other people to visit your profile page.

As you can see, Facebook will be able to create a great potential in internet marketing. The website already has the numbers in terms of traffic, and it also has the tools necessary for you to market your products or services effectively.

It is just a matter of knowing how to use these tools and also know how to effectively market your products or services. By creating a great profile page in Facebook, you can be sure that you will be able to attract a lot of targeted traffic.

Chapter 32: Facebook Marketing: Starting an Online Business

The newest trend in the internet today is joining one of the many social networking websites. Here, you will be able to keep in touch with your old friends as well as your relatives and you will also be able to make new friends as well as meet new people. With social networking websites, you will see that it will make the world a smaller place.

One social networking website that is so popular among many people from all over the world is Facebook. In this website, you will be able to post your pictures, discuss your interests and hobbies as well as do other great things.

In the past, Facebook was restricted to Harvard College students. In time, it expanded to other schools and universities until it became available for everyone above the age of 13 from different parts of the world.

Presently, the Facebook website now has more than 110 million active users worldwide.

Now, if you have an online business, you will see that Facebook can significantly help you promote your website and your business. Facebook marketing is now one of the hottest trends among online entrepreneurs today. Just think about it, with over 110 million active users worldwide, you will definitely have a lot of potential clients to do business with.

Because of the amount of people joining Facebook, a lot of online business owners are now joining this social networking website in order to market their products or services. With Facebook, you will definitely be able to effectively market your website.

The great thing about Facebook today is that anyone will now be able to join it. Whether you are a University student or you are an entrepreneur looking for a niche market, Facebook is the place that you should go to.

In fact, Facebook is now very popular that it is now investing a lot of money for advertising in order to attract more people to join. With this kind of benefit, you will see the potential on what your business can have.

Facebook as well as other social networking websites are now just beginning to see its full potential.

Today, you will see that Facebook has now launched its Facebook Ads system that will allow you and other fellow business owners to formally advertise your products and services. You have to consider the fact that people are three to five times more likely buy a particular product if their friends recommend it. If you advertise in Facebook, you will be able to increase your sales.

Facebook is now very popular that it now contains

ads for big corporations, such as Microsoft, Coca-Cola and other companies.

So, if you are thinking about marketing online for your business and you want to increase your company's sales, then you may want to try out Facebook. Here, you will be able to increase the advertising potential for your company. Also, you will be able to reach out to more people as well as get a niche market for your products and services.

So, if you think that online advertising or marketing is not working for you, you might want to try out marketing on Facebook. Here, you will be able to see how effective marketing is by using this one of a kind social networking website and you will be able to increase your sales.

Chapter 33: Conclusion

Marketing in a traditional sense has always been done by putting an ad either in the newspaper, the radio and the television.

Being in the digital age, efforts done by marketing to get the message across is not that different. It has just become a little more high tech which continues to help drive sales.

Businesses that want to sell something in the market need 2 things. The first is the product to be sold which later on will be distributed. The second is marketing which is the vehicle that is used to carry that message across to the consumer so that people are aware of its existence then it is purchased.

One way of the fastest ways of doing marketing today is building a website. Should one decide to shift and decide to do this, here are some online marketing tips one needs to know to get started.

1. The first thing to do is to determine what the person wants to do. The product has to fill a need that the customers want right now. It should provide a solution of some kind that will make that will improve the quality of life either at home or at work.

2. The next is to do the proper research. If the business is done with a group of people or a single proprietorship, it is best to brainstorm for the best domain name for the business. It should be catchy

and will easily be remembered by people. Given that there are probably other people who have been in the business longer and that it is possible that the domain name has already been taken, it is best to think of several names in case it can no longer be used.

There are sites in the web that have search engines to look for a specific subject and using popular keywords for ones website will easily help people find it. These sites also allow one to make a site map which can be downloaded in minutes for a small fee.

Another good example is the various email sites and by doing a tie-up with these companies, one can get exposure as well as free service since people who do not have an account can also sign up and be an active member.

3. A product of good quality should be sold at a decent price. Sometimes, the product one makes is already available in the market. To be competitive, one must figure out a way to convince people as to why this product is better than the other leading brands available. What features does it have that the competitor doesn't? What makes it unique which is not only about the product on hand but the service that this can give as well?

4. Just like having a normal business, one must acquire the right equipment and machines for the job. These could be merchandise that is either physical or electronic and an online ordering system.

To be successful, one should be sure that the goods

that a customer will order can be delivered on time. If there are any problems, a customer support staff or system should be ready to cater to that.

5. It takes money to make more money so one should be careful with what needs to be spent. By putting in tight controls in terms of expenditures and keeping track of the current balance while maintaining the same level of quality saves money which can be used for other things.

To avoid falling in this predicament, the first thing one must do is manage the expenses. It is always good to carry a notebook around to log whatever expenses have been made or have a logbook to keep track how much balance is left. That way, a person can stay within a budget on a monthly basis.

6. With everything in place, it is now time to promote the site. One can email to friends about the site and what it offers then this too will also be forwarded and advertised to others. Another is showcasing ones website in E-zines or electronic magazines to get more customer traffic.

Any business big or small must have the right resources available to get the message across to the people and building a web site or a site map takes time. One can do it alone if that person knows how to do it, get professional help or simply start from the basics and learn it from the ground up.

If you need help on this feel free to contact us via http://www.qualitywebdesign.aaglobalsourcing.com/

contact-quality-web-desig Your feedback is important to me.

Good Luck!

www.ingramcontent.com/pod-product-compliance
Lightning Source LLC
Chambersburg PA
CBHW051717170526
45167CB00002B/699